GOD IS YOUR PARTNER

✦

OTHER BOOKS BY JOHN-ROGER

Baraka
Blessings of Light
The Consciousness of Soul
Drugs
Dynamics of the Lower Self
Inner Worlds of Meditation
Journey of a Soul
Loving . . . Each Day
Manual on Using the Light
Master Chohans of the Color Rays
Passage Into Spirit
The Path to Mastership
Possessions, Projections, and Entities
The Power Within You
Relationships—The Art of Making Life Work
Sex, Spirit, and You
Signs of the Times
The Spiritual Family
The Spiritual Promise
The Way Out Book
Wealth and Higher Consciousness

With Peter McWilliams
LIFE 101
You Can't Afford the Luxury of a Negative Thought

For further information, please contact:
MSIA®
P.O. Box 3935, Los Angeles, CA 90051
213-737-4055

GOD IS YOUR PARTNER

JOHN-ROGER

Published by Mandeville Press
P.O. Box 3935, Los Angeles, California 90051

Printed in the United States of America

I.S.B.N. 0-914829-29-7

✦CONTENTS✦

FOREWORD

"SEEDING AND TITHING
ARE THE
LEFT AND RIGHT HANDS
OF GOD."

JOHN-ROGER

✦FOREWORD✦

✦ THERE IS A STORY TOLD OF A SOUL WHOSE time has finally come to enter into the world for what it hopes will be the last time. The Soul comes before the karmic board, which is the group that helps a Soul decide its life plan. The board looks at the Soul and says, "We have a very good life for you. In this life you are going to find someone who can take you back to God, and you will be able to lift from this world and go back to your true home in Spirit."

The Soul says, "Fantastic!"

The karmic board asks, "What is it worth to you?" and the Soul says, "To get off the planet? To go back to God? It's worth everything! I'll give it all!"

The karmic board looks at the Soul and says, "That's not necessary. All you need to do is give 10 percent."

The Soul says, "Ten percent? Last time I was on Earth, that's what I gave my agent. That's nothing!"

"Well," the karmic board says, "if you do give the 10 percent, you will be filled with so many blessings that you will not have room enough to receive all of them."

The Soul says, "Incredible! I give 10 percent, I find a spiritual teacher, I get tons of blessings, and I go back to God. What a deal! There must be a catch."

There's a moment of silence, and one of the elders on the karmic board looks at the Soul and says, "Yes, there is a catch.When you get down there, you won't want to do it."

So here we are on our way home to God, and many of us are saying, "I really don't want to tithe or seed."

Seeding and tithing are not requirements for participation in MSIA. In fact, as of the time of this writing, most people in MSIA don't tithe or seed. But the people who do are blessed with many gifts. It's a beautiful thing to do.

The financial level is the smallest part of this whole process. The biggest part is to open to the blessings of Spirit in your life and to know God in a greater way. And who could wish for a greater gift than to know God?

Paul Kaye
April 1990

SEEDING

"SEEDING IS
A SPIRITUAL ACTION
BECAUSE
GOD IS YOUR PARTNER."
JOHN-ROGER

✦1✦
THE DIFFERENCE BETWEEN SEEDING AND TITHING

✦ I AM GOING TO SUGGEST AN ANCIENT IDEA TO you that is for personal abundance. We could call it casting, "faithing," or seeding. Let me tell you how it works, especially in contrast to tithing.

In a way, tithing is asking, "What is the appropriate behavior in the eyes of the Lord?" It is saying, in essence, "God, thank you for what I have received. And from what I've received, I want to give 10 percent back to you." That's like an aftereffect: After I get it, I tithe. So, a very simple way of defining tithing, without going into the financial aspects of it, is your saying, "I am thankful for what I have already received."

Seeding is for a future-effect and is done beforehand. It works in the same sense as when you pray over your food and say, "Thank you, God, for what I am about to receive." With seeding, you are saying, "Before I receive this, I am acknowledging the presence of it."

When we seed and tithe, it's important that we pay attention to the attitude we're holding. We have to watch the thinking and the feelings and the body, because on this planet, we know that in terms of the polarity, there's more negativity than there is the positive. That's because the Soul is so positive that it has to have a tremendous balance of the negative polarity in order for it to stay here.

The tithing process is a statement that none of these "things" on the physical level belongs to any of us. If your attitude is, "I don't have money to tithe to the church," you'd probably better, because you may lose even what you have. Or, as it's stated in the Bible, "For everyone who has will be given more, and he will have an abundance. Whoever does not have, even what he has will be taken from him" (Matthew 25:29 NIV).

Now, we've seen people experience poverty in the midst of plenty, and their attitude is sometimes called "poverty consciousness." It's an attitude of, "I don't have enough, and there never will be enough." But listen, there is *endless* supply. Once you understand that, you are on your way to a much higher level of freedom.

One of the things that goes against seeding

and tithing is hoarding. We're vital, alive human beings, and part of our existence here is loving, caring, and sharing. Hoarding goes against that. Emotionally, it is a feeling of lack; financially, it's being miserly; physically, it manifests itself as disease.

When we start to place these blocks to abundance, we are out of line with our own spiritual directive—not the church's, not the Traveler's, our own. And when we're out of that, we can tithe and seed to bring ourselves back into alignment. We can come from all sorts of different levels and still be aligned toward God. But if we say we're aligned and we're not, we can have lack taking place inside of us. This lack could be feelings of unworthiness, or it could be where we don't have something and we say, "I don't have enough money. I don't have enough education. I don't have enough love. I don't have enough relationships." There it is—mental, emotional, physical lack.

Tithing is saying, "I give to God from what I have received." Tithing is a little bit under the law, and if you do it all under the law, you're bound. But if you do it through the grace of giving to increase things for everybody, an abundant supply comes to you in many different ways.

So technically, tithing comes under the law; it comes under the Old Testament. Seeding comes under grace as a future existence, and it's one of the most profound, best-kept secrets in the Bible. It has been called faith tithing, and we could also call it pre-tithing, except it's not based upon 10 percent of what you've received; it's based upon the amount you *want* to receive, and there's no limit to how it can come in. Still another name for it is the tenfold increase. For the bigger thinkers, it's called the hundredfold increase, and for the gigantic thinkers, it's called a millionfold increase.

Seeding is the idea of going to a field with wheat in your hand and casting it on the land as they did in biblical times. The implication is that there's an attitude of gratitude for having the opportunity of owning the land, seeding, and reaping. In modern times, when you're seeding for something in the future, it is not as clearly defined how that future event will be returned to you. This is in contrast to tithing, where you know exactly how it is returned because you have already received it.

Seeding says, "I know this future event will come through God's bounty." That could be money, better health, a change in job, and so on. How does God bring that to you? However God does it. And rarely does it come just exactly the way you expect it.

This idea of casting forward through seeding must include an act that commits you to it as a mental focus. You need a clear vision, a clear idea of how you want it to be, and you seed for that. Then you wait for the harvest—not in terms of sitting down but in terms of watering and fertilizing the ground so that there's something for it to grow out of. You make sure it's watered and fertilized by keeping your mind on what you want; you water and fertilize it out of your mental desires. It's an attitude or vision.

More simply said, seeding is the planting of what you want to receive, and tithing is the harvest. It's very hard for people to shake you loose from your Spirit if you've done both tithing and seeding because, in this process, God is giving to you and you're just giving back and saying, "Here, God. Here's some more." It's a phenomenal experience, but you may not know it until you try it. If you just take my word for it, you may never know. You have to do it for yourself.

Just do it if you're after the abundance and the prosperity and the harvest. When you get the harvest, you then share it through tithing, which is grace. And then you seed again with God as your partner, which is Divinity. You're recognizing the divinity of it all, the oneness of the whole thing.

Tithing educates the lower consciousness, and seeding is cooperation with the higher consciousness. Tithe for the lower self, seed for the high self, and share it out through the conscious self. Be the source of extreme abundance and overflow for everybody around you. In this way, you come back and reconnect your power with the glory of God.

✦2✦
PRINCIPLES
OF
SEEDING

✦ WHEN YOU ENTER INTO SEEDING, THERE ARE some key principles to keep in mind. If you're going to get a crop in the fall, what is the first thing you're going to have to do in the spring? Plant it. So you have to give first. You also have to know for what you're giving. If you plant rye, don't expect a horse. If you're planting wheat, don't expect rye. So to give first, there has to be a purpose for the giving: Why am I going to do this? And it's not an altruistic statement. It has to be a self-possessed type of statement: "I'm seeding because I want this." Then you lay out what you want.

When you seed, you need to do it with the real faith of the heart. You have to claim what you seed for, but you have to claim it in *God's* time and love. You also have to let God know that you're his "co-pilot," his partner. And although God is the "senior partner," you can't just seed and say, "I'll let God decide what to do," because God's *saying* to you, "You need to give me a blueprint."

If you say, "I want to reach that mountain over there," that's called imagining. But if you're doing the seeding, you start to prepare yourself *right here* to receive of the mountain. You check that the car has gas in it and that the tires have air. You check the road map to see how to get there, and the weather to see if you want to go at that time. With seeding, you must be able to see the mountain and see a way to get there. We hold clearly the inner picture of what we want, and then we seed for it. This is a fast way to personal abundance.

The idea is much like programming the universal mind. (And if you haven't heard the audio tape "Programming the Universal Mind," it would be a good idea to listen to it.) Get what you want as detailed as you can—as tasty as you can taste it, as smelly as you can smell it. As much as you can, activate hearing, seeing, feeling, tasting, and smelling. Then activate the intuitive sense, so that you just know. And all that will start working to pull in what you want.

You can also do a collage, or "treasure map," where you take pictures of what you're seeding toward and put them on a board, or you can create an ideal scene with the creative imagination, or you can use the technique of programming the universal mind, or you can use all of them. These things are all extremely valuable.

If you have made a treasure map or collage but it didn't work for you the way you wanted it to, it's probably because you also didn't seed for the things on it. You just envisioned what you wanted, and those things are still out there in your vision and never could show up. You have to make a path in order for them to come in, and they come in on dollars—or pesos or pounds, whatever is the medium of exchange.

If you want to seed for something intangible (for example, a relationship), you still need to put a value on it, and the only value we all can really agree upon is money, so you determine within you what that amount would be. Then you determine, again by going within, the amount to seed for the value you have placed on that intangible thing. If you want to seed for a spiritual quality, such as clarity, you have to see what clarity would be inside of you. If you think it is one thing and it's actually much higher, you may not get what you seeded for. Or you may get the higher quality because God might know the intention of your heart beyond your ability to say it.

Knowing *how* you're going to get there is not as critical as knowing *that* you're going to get there and, in that, not having any doubts, any second thoughts—nothing except the holding and the acting as though it is going to happen. This is not sitting and thinking as though it might happen, but *acting* as though it *is happening*.

You state what you want very clearly. Then you claim it as already being here, which is conditioning the consciousness. To receive, you need to act as though you have it; this is the faith statement that it is already present. You get your purpose clear, and if you get at cross-purposes with yourself, if you undermine your seeding with doubt, your seeding rots and decays. It doesn't bear good fruit.

It's very important that you do *not* tell *anyone* the goal you're seeding toward, that you are manifesting. Not your spouse, not your Siamese twin, because they can very subtly, through not seeing your vision, cast doubt upon what you've got. You'll buy their doubt as your own doubt even if you don't want to. Then when the negativity appears, they say, "See, I was right." Then you may say to yourself, "Gee, I wonder if they really are right." The god of opinion is now taking care of you and not the great abundant God. The god of opinion doesn't deliver abundance, health, and prosperity. It delivers rip down, tear down, and alienation. That's the law. The abundant God brings grace.

"As a man thinketh, in his heart he becomes." We're creators. We can create and see what we want and go for it. We can do the same thing negatively because this process of creation doesn't care what we go toward. If you get negative doubts and thoughts, the process will manifest those for you. So in undertaking seeding, you must understand that it's a real tightrope balance in terms of what you're going to keep holding in your mind. If you start getting negative pictures or thoughts about something you're seeding for, stop them immediately. Get up and walk around. Go work off the negativity with physical movement—throwing a baseball or running around the block. Then come back to what you want with a positive focus. You want to make sure you've got this thing going in the right direction all the time, and you have to watch your thoughts carefully.

There are parts of your consciousness that, if not addressed, will allow doubt to creep in. A little bit of doubt starts to grow into great negativity, until what you see is negativity. And the terrible news is that the doubt is also returned, based upon the principle "as you sow, so shall you reap." Some of you people have taken that seriously enough to say, "Do you mean that what I'm getting now is what I put out a long time ago?" Exactly. "How far back?" How long have you existed? "Well, I don't know." Since you don't know, start watching what you put out *now*. It's such a key principle to say, "You can't afford the luxury of a negative thought." It's extremely important.

You might ask, "Can I seed for a hundred

million dollars?" Absolutely. "Will I get it?" I don't know. Can you have that vision working so you can really see and feel it coming to you? If you can't, you probably won't be getting that.

You can seed for as many things as you can hold a clear picture of in your consciousness. You have to watch this because it's a pretty delicate balance that you're maintaining in yourself with your environment. If you get caught in the greed of it, then you get to receive of the greed, and you may not receive what you wanted. Then you live in lack: "I lack; therefore, I have greed." But if you have abundance, you don't have lack, and, therefore, you don't deal in greed. It often takes a while to transit across some of your old, habitual personality patterns, and seeding also assists you in getting free.

What do people get when they give? Sometimes, they just get the satisfaction of giving. Seeding has to give you the satisfaction of just doing it. You draw your picture and purposely design it. You tell it to God, and you release it to God. Then you go on about your business. And if you see something else you want, you seed again, and pretty soon the first one comes in and then the next. When does it come in? WHEN IT COMES IN. What if you don't get it within a certain period of time? I would say that if it doesn't start to return in about a month, look to yourself to see what happened. Maybe you need to be more patient. Maybe you need to seed again for that same thing. Go inside yourself to find out, because seeding is between you and God.

Energy follows thought. Thoughts persisted in produce the feeling in the heart and the character that we're going to be developing. So seed with the real faith of the heart. You have to claim it, but you have to claim it in *God's* time and love, which may not necessarily be yours. When you seed that way, with God as your partner, those things then take place. And the reason all this works is that you let go and give to God, joyfully and unconditionally.

✦3✦

SEEDING
TO
THE CHURCH

✦ WE'VE GOT PEOPLE WHO HAVE BEEN IN THIS church ten or fifteen years who are now millionaires from tithing. Someone recently said to me, "I would like to have more money so I can give more," so now I'm telling you about seeding.

This is the one that Jesus did. Do you want to know the occasion he did it? The multiplication of the fish and loaves is one of the greatest demonstrations of seeding. And what happened when it was all done? They had baskets full of what was left over—leftover, surplus, more than what people could eat, more than what was necessary.

We're to have abundance and prosperity, but in the past we never knew how to get it except under the law, which is "by the sweat of your brow." Seeding is under grace. We're giving it to the church and saying, "God is my unfailing supply. With God, all things are possible." What we're doing now is fulfilling the spiritual law of tithing, maintaining that, and keeping it because it's a commandment. And with seeding, we're also casting forward into the future as part of the vision of resurrection, or the re-creation.

There's no timeline on when you harvest what you seeded for because, in God, there's no time. When you seed, you are stating that the source of the harvest is *God*. You give the seeding to the church, but the church is not the one that is going to give back to you what you seeded for because we're not saying the church is God. We're saying God is God, and the church receives the seeding as the source of your spiritual teachings. Can you give it to other places? Yes, but it may not work as well. It may work somewhat, but you have to do more to make it work. By saying, "The church is the source of my spiritual teachings, and God is my source of all," you are involved in a sacred action.

You give to the church, you keep your eye on what you're going for, and if you have to take a circuitous route to get there, it may be because what you were after was in a different place than where you thought you saw it. On this alternate route, by-products that are blessings can appear. Are they a part of the blessings of seeding? *Definitely.*

Seeding the money to the church is saying, "I give to that which inside of me I hold as God's force on earth." That's a key thing to keep remembering. Can it work if you give it to a person? Yes, if you can see that person as God, or Divinity, or as the church, it can work that way. But most of us look at a person and find fault with them. So we'd rather give to a big organization for the greater good of all, and we call that the church. Does it have to be the Church of the Movement of Spiritual Inner Awareness? No, it can be another church. But if it doesn't work, try the Church of MSIA.

I'll tell you something interesting as an example. I wanted a palomino horse, and when I started looking for it, I must have seen six or seven pictures of possible horses. A good friend of mine was seeding to the church for me to get the palomino. (At that time, I only suspected that's what he was doing; he never told me, and I wasn't going to ask.)

One day, my friend said, "I think I know where the palomino is." We looked at some new pictures and said, "That's the one." The pictures were in the forest, and a lady was riding on the horse. We called up to get it, and the owner told us she had already taken a deposit from somebody else. My friend found this hard to accept and said, "Wait a minute. Offer her more."

I said, "That's not the way this works. We're not competing with anybody." So that horse went to the other people.

My friend told me a little while later, "I seeded for that horse. That was yours."

I said, "Tell me about the image you were holding."

So he told me, and I said, "You never saw me on the horse on the property."

He said, "No, I didn't. I just saw the horse for you."

I told him, "If it's for me, you've got to put me in the picture with the horse, and you've got to put both of us at Windermere." The next day we received a phone call about another horse, and we drove out to see it. We both looked and said, "That's the palomino." About a week later that horse was at Windermere, and I was riding it.

God is going to direct you in how to get the harvest that you have planted. Then here comes the real good news for the church. You seed to the church to get the money. You get what you want, and you tithe 10 percent of the increase. The church is going to get the seeding and the tithe, and you're going to get the bounty. That's a win—for you and for the church. And guess who the church is. All of us. The church money magnet becomes the money magnet for all of us, and the church's land becomes a money magnet for all of us, too.

You may be saying, "With tithing and seeding, the church is getting me coming and going." Right. But you're getting everything in between. And that everything in between is a tremendous amount. For example, let's say you seed $100 for a car, somebody gives you a $4,000 car, and then you tithe $400. That's giving $500 for a $4,000 car. I'd do that any day or every day.

Your relationship with God and your awareness of money and how you can relate to it and pull it to you can be either your restriction or your stepping-stone. You're called upon to make better use of your money, as well as your time, your thoughts, your feelings, and your direction.

With seeding, God is your partner, and that is the highest good that I know of. You're saying to God, "I'm giving it to this church as a way of giving it to you, and this church can use it for whatever they want to because this is the source of my spiritual teachings." If it doesn't work, talk to God, because he's the supplier. He set it up in the Bible. It's his scriptures, his word. Talk to him.

Take the message of what I've told you here and tell it to other people. The more people who are sowing for the harvest, the richer the valley will be. The storehouses will burst open, and a lot of people will benefit from what we're doing.

✦4✦

GOD IS
YOUR PARTNER

✦ YOU HAVE TO MAKE THE SEEDING ENOUGH SO
that you aren't saying, "Well, God, here's my
penny. Now give me a million dollars." Do you
think that's going to happen? If the answer is
no, then you know it won't happen, because you
can't get it into the core of your senses to bring
about a connection with it and pull it toward
you. It's your karma that you're dealing with
that sets it for you, and everybody's got their
own karma to deal with. But when you start to
have success with this, that karmic restriction
on your vision starts to leave because that success feeling goes, "Wow, I can enter into the
abundance of this."

There are stories where people have seeded

for money and the dollars didn't come, so they said, "It doesn't work." As soon as you negate it, guess what happens. It doesn't work. If you seed $35 hoping for $35,000, is that realistic? According to Divinity, it is. According to us? I don't know. Is it realistic inside *you?* If you can't make it realistic, guess what happens. That's your karma. That's the thing that stops it.

So the next principle deals with what we might call your karma. It's karmically written that some of you are never to be billionaires. Why? It would be detrimental to your spiritual progression. It is karmically written for some of you that you are not to be murderers because that's detrimental to your spiritual progression. It's also written for some of you that you are not to have great big apartment houses all over the world because it would be detrimental to your physical well-being. You would have to travel too much to take care of it all.

Along with the karma, there's also grace, and if we do seeding under the purpose and the principle that the Divinity has set forward to us, then it's handled by Divinity. Jesus said, "Seek ye first the kingdom of God, and his righteousness; and all these things shall be added unto you" (Matthew 6:33 KJV). That is the greatest seeding. But few people have the kind of contact with Divinity to trust it.

So you may wonder how you can trust Divinity more. How can you trust what you can't see? Well, who wakes you in the morning? Who breathes you all night long? Who drives the car when you're busy thinking of something else? Who does all these things for you? It's that part of us that is invisible, that, somehow, is always watching and aware and recording everything that's going on. If it records everything that's going on, then it can record only good if you put good forward. Get that purpose of "good" really clear because when your purpose is good, your purpose is also God.

God is your partner. That's the key principle that you've got to keep in mind. It's not John-Roger, not this person, not that person. It's God. In dealing with God, one thing you can't hold inside of you is resentment. If you hold some resentment, all your hours of faith seeding will give you back resentment. Or, even more important, the resentment negates everything so seeding doesn't seem to work for you, and then you get to have more resentment that it didn't work for you. It's not that you were rejected; you just resent that it didn't work.

As you seed and tithe, remember money as a divine energy of exchange. Money in itself does absolutely nothing for you. What the money can purchase for you is education, opportunity, recovery from illness, an increase in your ability to perform in the world, and so on. That's what money can do for you. Money itself also has no good or evil in it. So the question is, how do you use it? To your advantage or to your disadvantage? Use everything to your advantage, which is everybody's advancement. That's the key thing to get here. And know that when you enter into seeding, you receive of the grace of God's flow and abundance, and the bounty is amazing.

It's important that you are willing to receive of the bounty, however it comes in. Sometimes you will seed for one thing and get another thing. When it comes in, you may find that even though you don't want it, you sell it to someone else, and suddenly, the next thing appears, which is what you really wanted. That first thing had to come to you, then go back out, to eventually give you what you seeded for.

Faith seeding is powerful. The faith is claiming that you will receive prior to it coming to you. Faith is also basking in gratefulness for the grace of Divinity showered on you because you have seeded. And you did it joyfully.

Check to see if God keeps his word to you. And remember that the opening through which you give is the opening through which you receive. If you just fling wide the doors, what you can get will overflow to you.

✦5✦

SEEDING
STEP BY STEP

✦ WHAT FOLLOWS IS A SUMMARY OF WHAT TO DO when seeding:

1. Envision what you want or what you want more of in your life. See it clearly, see the details, see yourself carrying it out or living it. It can be a material item or something nonmaterial, such as a relationship, better health, etc.

2. You can seed for as many things as you want. However, if you are new to this, we recommend that you start with one area, so you can hold that focus and see it working.

3. Check your inner levels to make sure there is no doubt or second-guessing yourself.

This is very important because seeding can work as powerfully to reinforce your doubts as it can to validate your faith. We recommend that you tell no one about what you are seeding for. After you have received it, then you can decide whether you want to tell anyone.

4. When you see it clearly, put it in the Light for the highest good and make your claim. This claiming is the most important part and is the essence of seeding. It is beautifully summed up by Jesus the Christ when he said, "Therefore I tell you, whatever you ask for in prayer, believe that you have received it, and it will be yours" (Mark 11:24 NIV).

5. Now you are ready to seed by giving money to the source of your spiritual teachings. This will be the Church of the Movement of Spiritual Inner Awareness if you are a student of the Traveler's teachings, including being a minister or initiate. The money will generally be 10 percent of what you envision coming in (a tenfold return). But if you can handle the envisioning of it, maybe your return, now or in the future, can be a hundredfold or even a thousandfold. If you are seeding for something nonmaterial, we suggest you go within to find the dollar amount that represents a seed to you.

6. The final thing is that you give joyfully and with an attitude of gratitude for the blessings

that are already in your life. God is the source of your supply, and so you let go of any concerns about how you are going to get what you have seeded for. That is in God's hands, and God will bring it forward for you in his own timing and in his own way.

✦6✦

A STORY
OF
SEEDING

✦ DEAR JOHN-ROGER,

I have a great story to tell you. It's a story about seeding.

Back around December, about the time I received the letter about seeding, I was feeling that money was very scarce. My savings were decimated, partly because I had started paying for things that my parents usually covered for me (like school fees, books, some car insurance, etc.). They could no longer afford to do so because my dad, at that time, had been unemployed for well over a year. So while I understood why my expenses had increased, there was a constant battle in my mind. I was always thinking and saying, "I am so poor," or "I can't afford this."

Then later, not wanting energy to follow those thoughts, I'd affirm abundance, but soon I'd slip back into scarcity.

I figured that $500 would replenish my savings enough to make me feel abundant again. So I seeded 10 percent on that. But even before the $500 clicked in, things started changing.

On the advice of an inner voice, I checked out an old cigar box in my mother's bedroom for U.S. Savings Bonds in my name. I found $300 worth. I blessed my grandparents and aunts and uncles who had bought the bonds when I was little, and I cashed them in the next day.

I had intended to use the money from the bonds to pay for a general fee for the spring semester at school. But by a wonderful stroke of Spirit, I wasn't charged the fee.

My best friend, who had owed me a couple hundred dollars, got a high-paying job over Christmas break and was able to pay me back.

So at that point, I felt very thankful, very abundant, and I wasn't even looking for anything more.

Then, about three weeks ago, my literature professor called me. I had submitted (in December, actually) a research paper on Emily Dickinson to an expository writing contest. He called to tell me I had won first prize—a check for $500.

It was a wonderful, wonderful surprise. I really never expected to win that contest; I've never won anything. It felt like a week-long birthday. And for the first time in many months, I bought myself some presents.

And I also thought joyously, "Seeding works! It works!" I would like to say that I knew that all along, and I suppose part of me did. But the other part of me, the one that likes hard evidence, was especially satisfied.

A lot of other wonderful things have happened to me this year. I got a car (that's another great story I can tell you sometime). And this week, my dad got a job!

R.R.
Pennsylvania

✦7✦
QUESTIONS AND ANSWERS ON SEEDING

✦ *CAN I TELL MY SPOUSE ABOUT MY SEEDING IF we're sharing the same kind of vision?*

I suggest you don't tell anybody. I've heard a lot of people say, "My husband and I, or my wife and I, we share everything." And then they proceed to share the divorce. Since God is your partner in seeding—not me, not MSIA, but God—keep it between you and God.

I don't tell anybody anything until I've received what I seeded for. And when it's done, I say, "This is what we've done." There's no way anyone can put any negativity on it, psychically interrupt it, or mess me over, because it's done.

I'm seeding all the time. I have a lot of seedings

out there, but I also don't have more than what I can handle.

Remember, it's not this body, nor is it your body, that's rewarding us. It is you and God and how much contact you have with God, which is where s.e.'s are really important. Also important is the faith of seeing what you want coming in, seeing yourself receiving it, knowing you are going to get it. If you doubt it, the doubt goes into the seed, and you can get negative things coming forward. So this is why I say, don't tell *anybody*.

My wife and I are in a business partnership where we work together, and we want to seed together for the business because we do everything together for the business. Is that a different situation?

No, it is not. You can both seed for the business, but you don't tell each other the specifics of what you're seeding for. If you both say, "Well, let's seed for health, wealth, happiness, abundance, and more business," you can individually meditate on that. Then you send in your seeding money separately. If your spouse says to you, "What did you put into seeding?" you can say, "Darling, when it shows up, I'll show it to you." You see, it's between you and God, not between you and your partner here and God. When you seed, God is your *only* partner.

What's a good way to seed for a raise in pay?

If you want a pay increase of a thousand dollars, write it down on a piece of paper, and in the morning when you wake up, say, "I'm receiving the pay increase of a thousand dollars, and God is my partner in this." You enter into the feeling of it, the sensing of it, and then you let it go. You can do this for two days or more. And then when you have it clearly inside of you, you just let it go. At that point, it is in Divinity's hands. And when you let it go, you say, "God, it's in your hands. If I get it, you deliver it. If I don't, that seed is yours."

I know one person who did that and got fired from one job. He then went down the street to another company and got hired in the same type of position at an increased salary and with better working conditions. He also found the woman he eventually married.

I want to bring in a lot of money, but I don't have much. What should I do?

If you want a million dollars and you seed ten dollars for it, there is little practicality in that. You probably don't have enough power to attract the million dollars. A guideline is that it's a tenfold to hundredfold return on what you seed. So start from where you are, no matter how small, and build from that.

If it is a huge goal, should I seed for the huge goal or should I seed for the steps to the goal?

Why ask for a loaf of bread if you can ask for a grocery store? And a loaf of bread can be made up of many slices.

How do I seed for things that aren't material, that don't have a price tag?

Let's say you're seeding for a better relationship. I tell people to do an ideal scene of what that better relationship would be. Then close your eyes and go inside and ask yourself, "How much is this worth to me?" And inside of you, you spontaneously come up with a figure. You now have a value statement for yourself. Then say to yourself, "How much do I need to *seed* to make my ideal scene happen?" Then inside of you, you will get another figure. And you seed that figure for that value for that better relationship.

What if I seed for something, like a relationship, that's not really for my highest good?

It won't come in. But after a certain period of time (like three to six weeks), if nothing's moving, you say, "Thanks, God, for the relationship with you," because maybe that's what the relationship was all about. God says, "I don't want you to have anybody else. I want you to have me." Well, I'd settle for that. There's no question, because God is all things, including all the not things.

How many things can I seed for?

You can seed for as much as you can handle in your consciousness. And you seed for each thing separately. For example, if you want to come out to Conference in July, go to Jamaica a month later, and a month after that go to northern Illinois, then you seed for all three separately. Do not put them together as one seeding because if one doesn't come off, it blocks the other ones. So you seed for them as entirely separate things.

If God's my partner, can I just seed and let him decide what to do?

No, because he's saying to you, "Give me a blueprint of what you want." Your job is to provide God with the blueprint.

Is seeding a higher law than tithing?

Seeding is not a law. Seeding is done in cooperation with the high self, so if you're *only* seeding, the lower self can feel left out. So, as I said earlier, tithe for the lower self, seed for the high self, share it out through the conscious self, and be the source of abundance and overflow for everybody around you. Somebody might come up to you and say, "Oh, my God, my kid's teeth need fixing. I need a hundred dollars." You can say, "Here's your hundred dollars. You don't have to pay me back. Go get the kid's teeth fixed, and stop worrying about it so you can do your own seeding properly."

Regarding my money magnet, would it work to keep 10 percent of the money magnet and use 90 percent as seeding?

You can seed from the money magnet or you can tithe from the money magnet. I would seed from it because I'd be increasing my supply, my return, and I'd keep 10 percent.

When you tithe off your money magnet, you're tithing into the church magnet. When you're seeding, you're not necessarily seeding into the church magnet. You're seeding into God.

Would seeding be amplified if we as a group focused on the same thing?

Yes, but if somebody throws doubt into it, guess what happens. It's amplified doubt. That's why I keep telling you to come back and reconnect your power with the glory of God. This causes a conviction to appear inside of you that's so dynamic.

You see, I love this. I've done this for years, and I've never wanted to share it with anybody because I thought, "If I share this, it might be taken away." So I seeded for the giving away, and a year or so ago, it started coming up for me to share it.

Can I teach my kids to seed?

Yes. They get an allowance, so have them seed off the allowance. Seeding also teaches great money management. Kids start to realize, "I don't want to seed money for candy. I want to save it and seed it for this great big Christmas present." So they learn how to save and prepare, and they learn how to defer, to sacrifice for greater value.

I heard that if you have any doubts or negative thoughts, the seed would go negative. That's got me scared about seeding.

If you have doubt, which can cancel the seeding, and you don't get what you wanted, you can feel like you threw your money away. Then that stops you from seeding any more because you will think that it doesn't work. So you may say, "I'm not going to seed any more because I do it negatively." The solution is to grow up, learn to be mature, and handle it responsibly. There's no way to do this except to really do it.

What do you do with the human part that doubts?

In MSIA we deal in positive focus as opposed to positive thinking. With positive thinking, if you have a negative thought—poof!—there goes your positive thinking. Positive *focus* allows for negative thoughts along the way; you're just not sidetracked by them.

It's critical that at the time you seed, you're clear about what you are seeding for. That's your positive focus. It's important that there is no doubt present at that time because that doubt will cancel the seed. It'll put bugs in your harvest. That's why some people don't know how to work seeding. They're too interested in putting their focus into doubting.

Then, once you have seeded, if doubts come up, it's okay. Just let them go. However, don't focus on your doubts or be run by them because this will corrupt the clear inner vision, your positive focus on what you want.

It's like taking a seed of wheat and putting it in the ground and watering it. In two days you don't dig it up to see how it's growing. That kills it. You never get that seed back once you've seeded it. But after it produces the harvest, you can take part in the harvest.

It's very important that you take the harvest of the seed, or you can stop yourself from receiving the harvest—because what you take from the harvest is more seeds to plant for another harvest. If you plant wheat in the field and it comes up, if you don't harvest it, you will have no harvest next year. So you must receive of what you are sowing.

Personally, I don't put any negativity into my seeding. I just don't do it. You've got to find out for yourself how you don't do it. In fact, you have to find out for yourself how this entire process works. I'm just giving you some of the principles. It works so many diverse ways that there's no way I could begin to tell it all to you because it's each person's blueprint of his or her own karmic path of life.

If I seed for something and I change or I say, "That's not it," or it doesn't come in, is the seed still active?

Yes, but if you doubt that you can receive it, just forget it and start a whole new seed. Go from wheat to alfalfa. Don't go for a second field of wheat, which you've already poisoned by your own negative thoughts and feelings.

How is seeding connected to faith?

When you seed for something, you act as though you already have received it, which allows a space for it to come in. That's a form of "faithing." In the Bible, there's a story of a woman who reached out and touched Jesus' garment. This was a seeding action. She said, "If I touch his garment, I will be healed." It wasn't, "I touched his garment, and now I'm healed." She said it ahead of time, as an act of faith, which is the seeding process.

The principle says you get a tenfold to hundredfold return for what you seed. Then, on what you receive back, you tithe to the church, which is saying, "I got it. And thank you, Lord, for the harvest." Now you seed again. Your tithing is not a seeding. Seeding is a different thing inside of you, where you build the strength of your own faith and convictions.

Can I seed for someone else's health?

Absolutely. You do it just the same way you seed for anything else. You see their good health, you see them with vitality, the fullness of it, and you always do it for the highest good of all concerned. You send in the money—maybe it's five cents—and then all of a sudden their fingernails may straighten out, and you know that might not have been enough money.

Good health is an intangible, so you seed the amount you feel inside. It isn't necessarily a rational approach. It's more of an irrational thought, where you say, "This much will do it." Then you wait for three to six weeks. In about three weeks something should start moving. If not, all it says to *you* is that you did not do enough. So you send off some more seeding. In this case, it's still part of the original seed; you just didn't give enough to start with.

If you want something really big, you might seed so much every month for twelve months, until it reaches a certain point and the thing comes in. Or maybe it comes in along with something else.

There are so many ways this can work, and I don't know all of them. But I do know that it works according to *you*. I'd be really interested to have you try it and find out. And if it works, let us know, because we'll have more information about how to live this life better.

Can I talk about the thing I've seeded for if I don't actually say that I've seeded for it?

I wouldn't mess around with that. I'd keep that thing very sacred.

Can I write down what I'm seeding for?

Absolutely. In fact I suggest that you do write it down so that you can review it for about a week. Perhaps you can review it two or three times in the morning until you don't have to review it anymore because it's there inside of you.

Does it matter whether I give the money first and then later write it down?

Send the money first because then that makes you commit to doing it. If you write it down first, it's possible that you'll never get around to getting a perfect picture. You'll say, "Well, maybe this isn't quite right. I'll work on it a little while more." Send your seeding with the general idea of what it is, because God may read the intention of the heart and produce it for you within hours.

TITHING

"TITHING IS ABOUT
PLACING GOD FIRST
IN YOUR LIFE.

BEING A JOYFUL GIVER
IS A GREAT PART
OF LOVING THE LORD
WITH YOUR BODY, MIND, AND
SOUL."

JOHN-ROGER

✦8✦

ORIGINS

OF

TITHING

Then Melchizedek king of Salem brought out bread and wine. He was priest of God Most High, and he blessed Abram. . . . Then Abram gave him a tenth of everything (Genesis 14:18–20 NIV).

✦ WHEN THE PROPHET ABRAM (LATER ABRAHAM) was traveling home with the riches of battle after warring with a nearby king, he was met by a high priest in the order of God. This priest was Melchizedek, and it was at that time that the Priesthood of Melchizedek was established on the planet. Melchizedek was a direct radiation or emanation of the man who later came and was known as Jesus Christ.

The high priest in the order of God is Christ and is also referred to as the Messiah. As soon as Abraham saw Melchizedek, the wisdom of his heart knew he was seeing one who is with God. Abraham knew intuitively that he was to give back 10 percent of all that he had in the world to the representative of God, and so began the practice of tithing.

Melchizedek occupied the office of the Christ, as did some other prophets of the Old Testament. However, no one until the time of Jesus had the office of the Christ totally in one place at one time. When it is said that Christ is the only begotten Son of God, it means that God created one Soul energy and it went into all people. This means that we all have the elements of Christ within us.

When Abraham was blessed and then gave Melchizedek a tenth of everything, a spiritual covenant was set up for our time, whereby humankind is to give a tenth of its increase (what a person receives that is his or hers) back to God.

The above passage from the Bible may not sound like a covenant. But what it's not saying here is that there were hundreds of people around, and there was merrymaking, singing, praising, and hosannas. And there was all this booty laid out from the war Abraham had won.

The image you can get from the Bible is that two people met on a rock and shook hands. But it wasn't like that. This was flesh and blood, and when you put flesh and blood on the situation, you get that this was a major occurrence, an epic event.

As humankind fulfills its part of the covenant by giving 10 percent to God, then God fulfills his part by continually blessing us. God, of course, is always fulfilling his part anyway, so the question is, are *we* lining up, are *we* fulfilling the covenant?

People sometimes resist this process of giving their tithe. Interestingly, it doesn't belong to you in the first place; you are just restoring it to its rightful owner—God. Historically, people have tended to trust in materiality for their success. Instead of trusting in the Lord for their success, they trust in money or riches. Therefore, they withhold their tithes so they can have a lot more they can trust.

This happened to the ancient Hebrews, who, instead of being a pleasure to the Lord, sometimes turned to their own pleasures and stopped tithing. It wasn't too long before things went awry. When they questioned why, the answer was always that they had forsaken or given up on the Lord and that they had broken God's covenant. Then the people would restore the covenant by tithing; they would start to flourish again, and there would be no war.

Our job is to overcome our lower nature so we can live in the awareness of our Soul. When we tithe to the church or God, we are making the material world let go of us. So tithing is also part of a spiritual law and assists us in getting free of materialistic confinement.

In Malachi, it is asked, "'Will a man rob God? Yet you rob me . . . in tithes and offerings'" (Malachi 3:8 NIV). The question is, can God be robbed? No, but his covenant can be broken, and that is robbing God of the covenant. Later on in the same chapter, it is said, "'Bring the whole tithe into the storehouse. . . . Test me in this . . . and see if I will not throw open the floodgates of heaven and pour out so much blessing that you will not have room enough for it'" (Malachi 8:10 NIV).

When a person tithes, the universe that works under the spiritual law of tithing says, "If you have that much to give, that means you are open to receive more." In biblical times, people who tithed often received one hundredfold more than what they had given. When they received their hundredfold, they then gave 10 percent of that.

In MSIA many people know about the principle of tithing through my book, *Wealth and Higher Consciousness*. The book says that when we give to ourselves first, we tithe to the Christ within. Then, if we want to give to the church, we do that. If we want to build an organization, we tithe to the organization, and because we are part of the organization, we also get to receive of its wealth.

So, you may want to check it out with a joyful attitude of saying, "Lord, I am open to receive whatever it is that you bless me with." And then discover for yourself the blessing of fulfilling God's covenant.

✦9✦
LETTING GO

"Bring the whole tithe into the storehouse, that there may be food in my house. Test me in this," says the Lord Almighty, "and see if I will not throw open the floodgates of heaven and pour out so much blessing that you will not have room enough for it" (Malachi 3:10 NIV).

✦ ONE OF THE FUNDAMENTAL ERRORS THAT WE have as human beings is greed, which is manifested mostly in terms of money or monetary value. Greed, by its very nature, is a striking against the riches within oneself because it appears that there is never enough here in the world. Our eyes are always "hungry."

We can help to break the greed pattern by tithing, giving 10 percent of our personal wealth. When we tithe, two levels are activated—a level here in this world and, at the same time, a mystical, invisible level. The mystical is a communication saying, "You are abundant and handle abundance well, so here's some more." The other level, in this world, is when we look at our abundance and contribute joyfully through tithing. We are actually cheerful about it. This action sets up a countenance that is a form of glory in the human being, and that glory attracts more abundance.

When one person becomes free of materiality, it's like an infection going the other way. Instead of greed affecting honest people, honest people start affecting the greedy. You let go and give to God, joyfully and unconditionally. With people who say, "I don't have enough to tithe," I say, "Don't tithe," because their feelings of lack are telling them that they're going to need it. And with that attitude, they won't have enough anyway. Because they're hanging on, God can't supply them with more. They're holding on to it, scared to death about letting go of it. However, if they let go, they can rise to new heights inside themselves and get freer.

It's simple to tithe: you just give back 10 percent of what you earn to the source of your spiritual teachings. To those working with the Traveler Consciousness, this would be the Movement of Spiritual Inner Awareness. MSIA is a tax-exempt church, but tithing isn't done in terms of a tax deduction. It's done for the joy of giving. When you lovingly donate in this way, the abundance starts to come to you in many ways.

Tithing is actually a spiritual law: to give back to the source of your spiritual teachings. When you commit to doing it, something inside you works differently from that day forward.

Conditions may or may not immediately change in the physical, but inside, it can work wonders. And you finally own the Movement of Spiritual Inner Awareness. Before, it may have seemed like you couldn't really own it, like it was someplace in California, Chicago, or New York. When you tithe, you realize that it's *right here.* Wherever *you* are, that's the center.

I tell people, try it. Test it to see if it's true or not. Almost everybody who tithes keeps tithing because they say it works. The Bible says to tithe, to try God, and he'll pour blessings upon you. Some people think, "If I tithe, I'll get lots of money." That isn't what was said. It was said that God will pour blessings upon you. You may suddenly lose your headaches, or a backache may disappear. Or you may find that your spouse is getting along real well with you, or that the plumbing that was always getting stuck is no longer stuck, or that the person at the bank who was always hassling you has been transferred. These little miracles of perfect timing take place, and you say, "I can't believe this is all due to tithing." And I just tell people, "You have to check it out in order to know for yourself." I know for me.

✦10✦

IS TITHING BUYING GOD OFF?

✦ *Q: WHEN I TITHE, IT FEELS REALLY GOOD. IT just feels wonderful when I write the checks. However, when I attend a tithing evening or I talk about it with others, it feels like somehow I'm attempting to buy God off.*

A: In a sense, you really are. But you're not buying off some cosmic God. You're really addressing the God inside of yourself. It works almost the same way as doing things for your basic self, to get it to cooperate and to assist it in coming into line.

When you tithe, it is actually God buying *you* off, where God is the center of the universe bringing you into alignment by the process of tithing.

If you speak from your ego-center, saying, "I'm buying God off," it's absolutely a farce, it's ridiculous, and it cannot be done. That's like buying the air off. The air buys *you* off by giving itself to you.

Now, the negative power, which I suspect may put a word in your ear, will say, "This scam, this scheme, this conniving is just an attempt to get money from the people in a dishonest way, an unsatisfactory way, an underhanded way." The negative power has a lot of ways that it tries to do this. And usually it'll say, "And I don't have enough money to tithe. The kid needs shoes. I need this, I need that, I need this." And it turns you back to your materiality.

You can always tell when the negative power is doing that because it turns you to your lack. "How will I have the money to fly the plane to go do my spiritual work?" If you stop for a minute and look neutrally, you will realize that you put the material before the spiritual—because spiritual work can be done anywhere. So it's important that you watch the trickiness of the negative power because it can use your mind and emotions.

If the negative power came in with a pitchfork and a long tail and a red outfit, you'd go, "Aha! I know you. Get out of here!" But it comes in a most reasonable and well-mannered way. And its argument is your own argument, so it can very easily convince you or tempt you to your failure. To overcome it is simple. The real key is the joyfulness and the essence behind the giving.

The essence is so important. The tithe is recorded, but no one can record the essence, which to me is where I live and where I would like you to live because all that materiality goes by the wayside some way or other. It goes. But the essence is always present if we want to turn toward it.

✦11✦

A STORY
OF
TITHING

✦ DEAR JOHN-ROGER,

I am writing to share with you and my fellow ministers, initiates, and discourse subscribers about what my family has experienced since we began tithing.

Two years ago we were broke. We'd been living in a rent-controlled house for eight years and were suddenly evicted, leaving us (myself, my wife, and our seven children) faced with finding a new home. Rents had gone way up, and we had been just scraping by before. We felt desperate.

There seemed to be no solution. No one wanted to rent to a family with so many kids at any price, so in desperation I said to my wife,

"Let's start tithing. We're not able to meet our financial obligations anyway." Our phone had been shut off at least ten times in the previous two years for nonpayment, and I don't even know how many collection agencies were after us.

Anyway, we started tithing and, to make a long story short, miracle after miracle started to take place for us. And, less than two years later, we are living in a beautiful home (which we now own), and my wife has a new business that gives her more money and allows her more time off.

Before we started tithing, we owed thousands of dollars. Now we are free of debt and well in the black. I just felt it was important to let people know that tithing works.

B.Mc.
California

✦12✦
Questions and Answers on Tithing

✦ *Why should I tithe?*

There are no shoulds to tithing. You may, however, wish to open up a channel of greater abundance for yourself, and tithing is an effective and proven way of doing this. The abundance comes through Spirit and takes many forms. Remember, you are tithing for *you*, for your own growth and upliftment.

Why do you suggest I tithe to MSIA?

If you actively study Soul Awareness Discourses, MSIA is likely to be the source of your spiritual teachings. In giving to MSIA, you are, essentially, giving to yourself because you are part of it. MSIA then gives back to you through the dissemination of spiritual teachings and through having physical locations, such as Prana, Arrowhead, and Windermere, where you can go for spiritual renewal.

I am on discourses, and I am studying toward initiation. I also go to church, which I often find inspiring. Can I give 5 percent to my church and 5 percent to MSIA?

A person will usually have one source for their spiritual teachings. What seems like another source is often a form of fellowship or support. Therefore, we recommend that you decide what your source is and give the full tithe to that.

I'm confused. Do I tithe on the money I receive net (after taxes) or gross (before taxes)? It seems like I've heard of both being done.

When you tithe to yourself, you tithe on the net amount of money you receive. When you tithe to the source of your spiritual teachings, you tithe on the gross (before taking out taxes), the idea being that you give to God before you give to the tax collector.

Is tithing tax-deductible?

Although MSIA is a tax-exempt organization and tithing qualifies as a contribution, many people have decided not to claim their tithes as tax deductions. This is because the money they tithe does not belong to them in the first place; it is God's, and they prefer to have their blessings come through grace rather than have the reward come through a tax deduction. Of course, it is up to you to decide what you want to do, since tithing is a matter between you and God.

I received a car as a birthday present. Someone mentioned that I needed to tithe on the value of the car. I don't think this is correct since I didn't receive any money. Am I right?

No, you are not correct. You tithe on your increase (anything that is added to you). This means that you tithe not only on money but also on the value of gifts you receive. This does not include loans, since this is not an increase because you owe the money. However, if the loan is forgiven, you would tithe on the forgiven portion.

You mean that if I receive a shirt as a gift, I tithe the value of that?

Yes, since the shirt is your increase. The attitude

here is one of gratitude for the gift. People who have really lined up with tithing find that the blessings line up right behind them.

I stopped tithing and have found myself living in lack, and now I want to tithe again. Is there anything I have to do to renew my commitment?

The commitment or covenant is between you and God, so the act of tithing renews the covenant automatically. Because of the sacredness of this covenant, it is important to bring yourself back into the flow of tithing by tithing from the time you *chose* to start tithing again up to the time you actually *send in* the tithe. For example, if you recommit to tithing on March 15 and send in your first tithe on July 1, you would make sure you have tithed on all your increase from March 15 to July 1.

Is it okay to miss a tithe? I sometimes get insecure about the large bills I have to pay.

Let's look at it this way: By tithing, you have set up a channel for God's abundance. This abundance comes through in Spirit's timing. Why not keep this channel of blessings continuously open? Your tithing is your statement that you are open to receive. Tithing works from inside you, so you may want to sacrifice your insecurity for the joy that comes with giving. As Jesus said, "The harvest is plentiful, but the laborers are few" (Luke 10:2 RSV).

Do you suggest making tithing a lifelong habit?

Yes. Tithing is easier when it is done regularly upon receipt of income. An attitude of gratitude will usually come present as 10 percent is given to Spirit. As regular tithers have found, the blessings do pour forward, even in the testing times. This demonstrates that Spirit keeps its promise to us for life; all we are doing is choosing back.

My husband recently lost his job, and we are short of funds. Shall we tithe?

Yes. Tithing has to do with your personal relationship with God. Tithing with the correct attitude is an affirmation of that relationship. It has been set up for you to receive of God's abundance. There are often tests, but if you stick with it, you will probably be writing a success story for the *Tithing Times*.

I don't work, and I don't bring in any money. All the money I get is from my husband's work. And when he gives me money for the supermarket, I tithe 10 percent of that. Is that all right?

It's not really because that's not an *increase* to you. That's the supply for the family. If he gives you money for you, then I'd tithe on that. The money he gives you to buy food is not a personal increase. You're just acting as a steward, taking the money and buying supplies for the household.

What if he gives me money for clothing?

That would be different because that's your increase. However, if you're buying clothing for the other members of the family, that's not your increase. That's for the group's increase.

I've been tithing on my gross salary. I also get a lot of benefits from my company, like medical insurance and dental insurance. Do I tithe on that, too?

No, that's not an increase to you. It's a benefit to you. You don't get it. You can't tithe on what you don't get.

So you wouldn't consider that a gift?

No, because I haven't used the medical insurance plan or had my teeth fixed, or my car hasn't wrecked in ten years, so what's the increase?

What if I go to the doctor and I get 80 percent of the fees covered by the insurance company?

It's not an increase. You never saw it; it went to the doctor. If the insurance company paid 110 percent, you got a 10-percent increase and you would tithe on that amount.

I was in a car accident, and I've been reimbursed for the medical expenses.

That's not an increase. It's matching funds that went out. If you get a loss settlement, above and beyond it, that's an increase. If you have to use that money to fix your car because of the damage from the accident, that's not an increase.

Just to be clear on the tax deductions: Say I deduct a donation to a university. Is the amount of the tax savings that I receive an increase?

No, that's not an increase because you have already tithed on the gross amount of income that you received.

So, if I go to a chiropractor and he doesn't charge me, would that be an increase?

Technically, if you receive lasting benefit

from going to him and he would have charged $40 and he didn't charge you and you receive the benefit of healing and health from the chiropractic adjustment, $4 is tithed.

When I first started tithing, within three weeks to the day, all this negativity came on me and it was like, "I don't have enough money for this, and I don't have enough money for that." So I tithed a double tithe, and the next week I made precisely that amount of money.

I've never talked about double-portion tithing, but you just now brought it up. That is really creating more abundance.

Thanks to you, J-R, I knew what was going on when all the feelings of lack came up. I had the wit to recognize the negative power on me. So I went double time, and from that point on I've also been doing two hours of s.e.'s with no problem.

Isn't that a great thing? You know it in yourself. Well, God bless you for doing it, because that's where the blessing sits.

Should I keep a money magnet, or should I tithe?

The optimum thing is to do both. However, if you were to do only one, I would suggest you tithe. Donations are man's law, tithing is spiritual law, and the money magnet is a law unto yourself.

Why is it that when I tithe to the money magnet, it's on my net income and when I tithe to MSIA, it's on my gross income?

The gross represents the totality of Spirit; it's what God has given to you. The net represents what you use for your own Soul development.

I'm in business for myself. On what amount do I tithe?

There are two things to look at here. First, there is your salary or what you draw from the business, and you would tithe on the gross amount of that. Then there is the profit the business makes. If you were in biblical times and you sold a horse, you would tithe on the increase, which would be the selling price of the horse less the cost of the horse. If we take that into modern times, you would probably tithe on the difference between the selling price of your goods and the cost of those goods to you. This is sometimes called the gross profit.

What if I am a lawyer?

Then you would probably tithe on your gross income.

Can I deduct overhead expenses in computing my tithe?

Technically speaking, no. However, it's up to you because you're the one tithing. I can only present the guidelines. Tithing is between you and God, and the most important thing is that you do it joyfully and unconditionally. God knows the intention of your heart. So the key is to keep things straight in your heart and you'll be fine.

What if I am given a scholarship or somebody gives me a room to stay in free of charge. Do I tithe on that?

Technically, yes, but on the value placed on it.

What if I don't have the money?

If you have no money, then obviously you can't tithe. But I know from observing people who tithe regularly and with the joyful attitude that they always have the money, and the blessings are pouring forth for them. You see, tithing is about putting God first in your life. Put God first in your life, and you can count on God doing his part. You will know in your heart what you are to do. Trust that and don't hassle yourself.

I tithe and I give just because, to me, that 10 percent is God's. I just write out my check, and I don't think about being joyful or anything else because that's God's, and there's not too much to think about. Is that being a joyful giver?

Yes. Joyful giving isn't doing, "Yay, team! Cheer, cheer, cheer! Fight for the Lord until you die. Rah, rah, rah!" It is the essence of what is in your heart that counts.

WHAT'S NEXT?

"IT'S VERY HARD FOR PEOPLE
TO SHAKE YOU LOOSE
FROM YOUR SPIRIT
IF YOU'VE DONE BOTH
TITHING AND SEEDING."

JOHN-ROGER

✦WHAT'S NEXT?✦

✦ IF YOU WOULD LIKE TO SEED OR TITHE, ALL you need to do is send a check or money order to the Church of the Movement of Spiritual Inner Awareness (MSIA) at the address below.

If it is a seed, please mark that on your check, but do *not* put what you are seeding for. We can send you a supply of "God Is My Partner" seeding envelopes if you would like to seed regularly. Just let us know.

If you would like to tithe on a regular basis, we can send you "I Am a Joyful Giver" envelopes upon request. We can also send you a tithing commitment card. Your commitment to tithe is between you and God, and the card can assist you in supporting this commitment at the basic-self level.

Please feel free to call the MSIA office if you have any further questions on seeding or tithing. And may you be filled with God's blessings.

MSIA
P.O. Box 3935
Los Angeles, CA 900 51
213-737-4055

ABOUT THE AUTHOR

JOHN-ROGER, an educator, has traveled the world teaching, lecturing, writing, and presenting seminars on personal and spiritual growth. He is the founder of a number of organizations that support such endeavors as education, personal growth, divinity, philosophy, health, service, integrity, business excellence, and individual and world peace. He has written over 20 books, recorded hundreds of audio and video seminars, and has a nationally seen television show, *That Which Is*.

Through his unique ability to recognize the spiritual reality in day-to-day situations, he has assisted thousands of people throughout the world toward a healthy, happy, and wealthy way of life.